D1432367

OTHER PEOPLE'S COMFORT KEEPS ME UP AT NIGHT

Morgan Parker

SWITCHBACK BOOKS
CHICAGO

ISBN-13: 978-0-9861876-1-2

ISBN-10: 0986187615

Library of Congress Control Number: 2015933637

Book design: Elle Collins

Cover art adapted from work by Sam Vernon.

Switchback Books

Hanna Andrews, Founding Editor

S. Whitney Holmes, Executive Director and Editor

Colleen O'Connor, Managing Editor

editors@switchbackbooks.com

www.switchbackbooks.com

TABLE OF CONTENTS

THERE ARE OTHER THINGS I WANT TO EXPLAIN BUT THEY ARE MYSTERIES

What is usually said about love I ignore
worship instead the wilted flowers gleaming
in our throats what you don't know is
I envy this world and I want to save it
squeeze its bloodied hand like so
saying this will sting but only for a minute
our primary concern will always be
the gnawing feeling like when I wake up
to wonder how many serial killers have entered
my life how the truth can feel like
ant hills their sandy curves their tiny crests
like nipples what I really want to ask is
what do you think of the idea of progress
and is it an injury I can fix

The World Is Beautiful but You Are Not in It

Let me refer to myself in glorious ways:
Colors seem brighter, the sky is a shocking blue.

I carry my stomach in this bowl
and earth is planted in my blood.

From your last letter, I gather hills.
I'm trying to keep my tenderness in check.

Trying to see what kind of grill the neighbors have
is everything I couldn't do before.

Now brown eggs shift heavy in my palms, this bowl.
Words make their way up my thigh.

I swear very nice boy and I refer to myself.
No. The hills are holding you and I refer to myself.

Let's be honest: I need a real man, I say out loud.
Every weakness I have settles into a tree trunk,

stays all winter. I don't know if I mean it.
Winter has lasted five years already.

This morning I press into the edges of my stomach.
My mother makes coffee in California.

Ladies will say we are expert with machines
but they will be under two pitchers of sangria.

I said you could make music out of this.
Ingesting artificial palm trees, exploding.

Your letters are getting shorter. I am getting close
enough to the sun to touch the tip of its cigar.

We carry what is shocking and heavy in blood.
Music seems brighter: the sky the sky.

IF MY HOUSEMATE FUCKS WITH ME I WOULD GET SO REAL (AUDITION TAPE TAKE 1)

I didn't come here to make friends.
Buildings spit their stomachs at me
and I spit back, down the sidewalk
into a bitch's hair. I am a forehead
careening in clouds, a dirty tree branch
brushing against the shingles
of the production room. I am
groundbreaking: two as one.
Brooding tattooed over my art.
Otherwise, black.
Can do angry, can't do
accents. I need little coaching or
provocation. Opinionated and
everything a man wants.
Lips and boobs camera-ready.
If I hear you're talking shit about me
in your confessional interview,
please know
seven birds have fallen dead at my feet
right out of the sky.
I learned this right hook here
when I was only six. Bitch, please.
I'm so real my hair is going gray,
legs bruised up like tree bark,
veins of my neck as swollen as
ripe fruit, the cheeks of what is growing.

FACE CATHEDRAL

Blues songs are how I feel
when I let strangers
use my lighter. Already
traffic on the expressway.
Plants in rows
like apartments.
In Africa this man
is a lawyer
but here
he sells records
on the street.
He says, *Everyone is so quick*
to tell the world
about their
problems but
they won't
tell a priest. He says
he needs a woman
with hollow cheeks.
By now, only imprints
of flowers. Knobs
in the trees,
swollen faces.
When dogs look at me
as they pass I imagine
they are ancestors
watching.
This is the difference
between fog
in the skyline
and me, or a steamboat
frozen on the river.
The trumpet solo
is your face
in a new world.
Confessions heard
in English, Spanish, Portuguese,
and sticks
on wood.

POEM FOR THE JUNE ECLIPSE

I'm glad the black girl
got a line in this episode

I'm glad the universe
isn't about my people

We nothing but half-finished
tattoos: ladybugs to the eardrum

Don't you think this eclipse
lasted a little too long?

Number three and this should
definitely be number one:

Never get high
in the bedrooms of your friends

I just hope the ground doesn't freeze up
before you clench that jawline of yours

Something cascading outside answers
Frankly, it's a voice I don't trust

You: crying in a theater
You: Rorschach of a face

Three apples on the counter
are touching at the hips

Lemme sit up in your half-moon
even if this isn't what it's all about

MISS BLACK AMERICA

Does she drink   smoke lights
Does she bother spitting her seeds

Does she hate   her little sister
Is her ringtone R-E-S-P-E-C-T

Does she wake up next to you
and shudder

Does she think she's crazy
Does she go to church

Does her therapist ask
where her desires have gone

Does she know
what makes her special

Does she say wild
and free   does she believe it

Poem Made of Chewed-Up Nicorette from the Garbage in Front of Kate Hudson's House

Getting dressed for the day, I find mold
in an old coffee cup. What I mean to say is this:
Honesty is uncomfortable and funny.
For example, today is whiskey sour day
and I know this. I return to the fields
to measure and cut the thatch that houses Kate Hudson,
her lizards, and her addiction to sucking toes.
I do not know who I am while I am doing these things.

Dreams are sex and towers.
Freshly cut grass nowhere except brain tunnels.
In the morning you roll over and tell me
there is something to be said
about the last one in the pool, unassuming DJ names,
and folks with imprints on diner stools.
These are all of my personas. You love
broken skin the way I want to punch liars in the face.

In these ways I am like Kate Hudson:
Aren't men a bitch? Aren't they all just dicks?
We both orgasm last
and get together with girlfriends to discuss text messages.
Beautiful women are as underappreciated
as the rising price of a pack of Virginia Slims.
In a bar somewhere she raises her glass and whispers to me:
The whole world is my bedroom.
Three birds nestle their wings into her thatched hairs.
Nature makes itself horizontal. No adventures, just
soup for dinner. And I want to know
what's really going on in your coffee, sir.

This is how to brush and trim the thatch,
make it feel important.
This is not a method for relieving sexual tension.
It is a resting place for Indonesian cigarette butts
and rusted nails. The day is vast and smothers me.
Also: things lined up quite nicely without a temper.
And: below the surface of my veins.

Real Housewife Defends Herself in Front of a Live Studio Audience

In response to Barbara from Florida: Who doesn't love
an educated mistress? We ladies
know how to get airtime. They're fake,
by the way. But I don't want to start drama.
When she said that I was like, you're just jealous
I have a hit song, and new money

just wants to be newer money.
I love
to go out for cocktails with the ladies
when I get lonely in this big house, fake
a buzz, sit back and watch the drama
unfold. Are you jealous

of my yacht or are you jealous
of my husband? I married for money.
I mean love.
Queens of suburbia, we are the ladies
you want to be. Our cheeks aren't fake,
just enhanced: valleys where fingers dramatically

brush away straightened hair. We eat drama
out of the tabloids for dinner, take jealousy
under our tongues with pinot grigio. Money
can buy class, nannies, diamond rocks to love
and die for. To behave like a lady
is to restrain oneself from pulling fake

hair extensions out of the head of a fake-
ass bitch, and for that matter, any drama
in the parking lot of a banquet hall, any jealous
glasses sent into orbit. Remember that money
is security, a hairless cat to hold and love.
To use. To want more of. Ladies,

we look damn good spending it. Ladies,
this makes us powerful. Listen, just fake
an orgasm if you need to with a few dramatic
moans. You're here to make the other husbands jealous.
Take a look at this rack. You think my money
came from god? Keep a vague idea of love

in the breast pocket of your fake fur coat. By love,
I mean a cul-de-sac without drama, a weekend away, how money
makes you feel down there. Do you feel it yet, ladies? Are you jealous?

How to Piss in Public and Maintain Femininity

is the name of a course I am teaching now
in church gardens downtown and under SUVs
in LA after a club with a name I do not remember
just like Queens last night which was a trip so I walked
off the strangeness for over an hour before
I called you which I now know was ill-advised
but at the moment felt inevitable what with
the martinis and the way I want what I want
regardless of social etiquette and the way
I am ashamed of my unconscious by which I mean
I never fucking learn my lesson
I say everything out loud

I am always thinking of sex and sleeping with
no room left in the bed I am always thinking
of sex or theorizing about sports and board games
and how they are the reason I am alone
a soldier always thinking of these differences
tiny birds line the sidewalk in front of my building or
someone comes into bed with me and we get
a good night's sleep while the alarm clock
glows in another direction

Somewhere we are honest
I cry and it makes me sleepy
turns grass into a lighter shade of brown
the small difference between think and touch
black music is not a folk tale it is
a rounded coffee pot this morning
you are well versed in deceit
sometimes I forget I have tattoos
I pretend things are simple but I do this
for your benefit watch Nick suck
on the pit of an avocado as if
this is what we have been waiting for

when I think I hear wind chimes it is
only a car alarm when I say
I will write you it stands for something else
Matthew McConaughey is that you
in my bed but you are not singing
you understand there will be morning

there will be a silly war and I'm like
boy how did you get in my bed
and why aren't you singing?

I remember everything especially
the way you never let me speak
what is off-key will wake me up in the morning
when I say I will write you
you represents something else and larger
in the morning I feel my stomach
I press into its edges and experiment with control
I wake up before I see who wins me back

The Housecleaners, Early Wednesday Morning Downtown
after Gwendolyn

Cinderella jams to Curtis Mayfield
while scrubbing her
own vomit from the bathroom
tiles. On her hands and knees
she's all like,
Damn why
I gotta be the man of the house?
A ghetto child is defined
by time
not as valuable as other time.
It isn't vomit but
it might as well be. I watch
Cinderella bob and hum
scraping roommate's hair from the drain.
We/ squeeze sponge, she says,
showing me the way.
There might be a prince, but homegirl
does not remember.
She doesn't remember anything
after midnight.
Real cool like:
We smoke
whatever we can get our hands on.
We go downstairs,
brush from our necks a smell
like honey burned into the bottom of a pan.

MORGAN WHAT, MORGAN WHO?
"Do not bark up that tree. That tree will fall on you." -Jay Z

Yes and I am
dreading the new year
I say to my mother
on Christmas when she asks
if I am really
that bitter. I spit
at the nickname
you hand me—a kink
in vinyl where
needle sticks
and repeats between
my legs. Leaving my lips
you're cheap liquor
lusty and sad
over my blueprint.
Peep all these inches
left un-bruised, crowned
with dried leaves
and spilling
out of my shirt.
I have an appetite, make
light posts go down when you
call me baby. Baby, don't
forget who's quitting who,
who is harvested
and who sows.
Careful with that
face of yours: You know
this weather
is my fault.
Trains get lost, roads flood
worry and charcoal.
Motherfuckers
better duck.

MISS BLACK AMERICA

Does she grind slow
on back-when harmonies

squint at Boyz II Men high notes
or mosh-pit in shit-kickers

Is she   a flower in your mind
Is she bootylicious

Did her mama say
there'd be days like this

Is she rhythm
or blues   Billie   or Billie Jean

Do the white boys back it up
Are their mothers terrified

I'm Not Like the King of Black People

I'm sorry I don't
know why I like
grape soda or how
my hair got like this

I couldn't tell you
where the watermelon
thing came from

I'm what
you don't swallow
the glossy   dark

I read somewhere
my folks used to be princes
their earrings were
pulled out
in their sleep

then one day
they woke up

eyes red and blue
craving chicken
and gold teeth

*

If you are quiet
for long enough
you can hear

my stomach
fill with color

chariots and rivers
in a language
you will never
understand

what got buried
under Kentucky bluegrass
slit open

like the side of a hog
whose backs
swelled up

became the pink
of my gums

*

It happened that I became
the same as
shoe polish   low-grade fever
you can catch

staring too long
at the moon
or falling asleep
to Etta James

your body
can't be a cure

let me
spoon-feed you
acrylic nails
jukeboxes
while you sweat

let me press
my cold tongue
to your head

*

I read somewhere
my blood is gin
and OJ from the carton

my people
just words
in damp soil

one day they got
scuffed onto
a wooden block

melted into tar
and troubled
water

then someone
leaned back
on a plastic-covered
sofa   lit

a menthol   I was
discovered
a red circle
around the filter

It Doesn't Get Cold Where We're from and We Weren't Taught

One day, thought I left the ground.
My body, a tufted edge
          wrapped in neon   and what the Bible says
I felt you—
orange scraped blacktop like
a yawn curled
against clicking teeth.
Of submission   many ways.

I am worried
angels are in my room
          breathing.

What were we taught, exactly? To navigate
and withhold. To get sick.
I'm thinking,   *pressed up against*, and
what about my father and his fathers
          fishing men
          and fists.
We are examples of paper.

Say goodbye to Daddy   he has plans.
I am damned
I have hopeless feet.

Real Housewife Considers Feminist Theory While Sketching Designs for Her Handbag Line

Any woman knows
the math of luxury.
The handbag is a symbol:
my privilege
my man.
My man is plastic
money.
The purse is my uterus.
Who's holding who?
Luxury handbags will save us.
Luxury handbags
and leather mystique.
Luxury handbags filled
with lists of men
I wish I loved.
Tiny dogs piss on new trees.
Daughters go to college.
Suburbs are luxe and orange.
I join Twitter.
I break the plastic ceiling.
I am a privilege.
My pleasure
snakes at his feet.
I throw shade and sip tea.
My small plastic
mouth. My plastic neck.
I strip down to a woman.
What is a woman?
Women
are a problem with a name. Girl,
bye.
Power is money and my body
glistens.

I Was Trotting Along and Suddenly

The wind blew two empty
beautiful cans of Four Loko
past my loafers so I took
a picture with my phone
and sent it to Ted as found art.
He didn't respond. The evidence
was nestled in a bed of leaves.
I was in no hurry to grow older
and understand you so I stopped
to watch a mysterious car being towed,
leaned against three swooning
bikes like a casual Dalmatian.
The sky was acting exactly like
my mind: taking in the same quickness
day by day, always about to rain
over traffic cones. If my words today
were not airless flags, they would be
something you don't hope for
but wonder about years later.
Like the false sense of intimacy
in falling asleep next to strangers
on the L train. I'm more inclined
to Timberlake than Plath, and I like
to get stoned, make my stomach
a living drum. I'd let down my hair
if I had any, step out of the golden
barbershop fresh as a cold pear.
There is no snow in California
but my mother says there are laws,
and Sean says something about
how he is only a myth.
I'm at parties acting perfectly a fool.
Past my cheek the wind blew some soil
resurrected from a pale flower pot.
Then I ate a hot dog for lunch
which was better than I expected.

BOYS, BOYS, BOYS
after Jay Z

Got homies
in the Deep South and two parts of Newark, bartenders
in the East Village and West,
      white-walled bedrooms, their mamas' cribs
      writing love letters, blowing up my cell
making promises sweet
as B-sides to take me to St. Tropez,
to jump
when my drink looks low.

In California, the dudes
are so cute they're stupid, smash Nattys
on the sides of their skulls, get me
high in backseats and the corners
of suburban house parties.

For years I've been scattering them:
blue-eyed men
coloring one side of the sun,
long-haired guys sweaty with treble,
      hustlers with shiny rims for teeth,
      running always from wild plants and police.

Applicants without extensive
dicks and cash flows need
to sit the fuck down.
      Everyone else, you alright, except
      I'll expect you to change for me.
I know you won't, I whisper
to every boy every morning
while he snores, stiff
and hairy in my bed.

I'll take whatever, but: New kicks
better be so fly I lose my breath.

The wanting more
can make a sister crazy so I settle
for free shit: Trade you digits for dinner
and treat this like the business it is.
I can make a mixtape my own
damn self.

Poem Made of Empty Prescription Bottles from the Garbage in Front of Bill Murray's House

"Take dead aim on the rich boys. Get them in the crosshairs and take them down."
–Bill Murray as Herman Blume, Rushmore

I fall into a green pool, take the leaves with me.
What I mean: Accidentally sad
is the same as very funny.
The roads here are slick and dark.
Bill slips on a bar stool. We are
the only two people.
We say our names
are what they aren't.
He steals the cigarettes while I'm
not looking, tucks his empty bottles
into couch cushions. We are in the shit.
This is called black
powder. A sprawl of roads
we survey from a hill.
Rich Boys are circling
like bonfires on the shore.
No pink flowers in their hands.
We are not going somewhere, Bill Murray
and I, spoonfuls of gray
light in our hands.
I'm a little bit
lonely these days
except for unfiltereds
and bourbon on rocks.
I am everybody-consuming. Still
very small and afraid
to answer the phone.
Is that you, future Morgan,
calling from Long Island breathing
humble disaster
I should avoid today?
I open my mouth but no one is there waiting.
When I call back, the numbers are only zeros.
I am obsessed
with the future, which is greatness
but also vomit and leaves
to fill the hole, something
too soft for the backs of our heads.
Bill is humming:
I feel good I feel

great I feel wonderful.
Meanwhile I'm weeping into free edamame.
They've led
a hard life, the Rich Boys.
It's something about how
their eyes say nothing,
is why I want to fuck them.
Sometimes a black raincoat
comes into my dreams
too foggy to be anyone.
I fight with my legs, kicks
I never knew I had.

America This Is for You
(Audition Tape Take 2)

Let's talk for a minute
about how many free shots I can expect. Because if
it's like, ten per night, sure—
I'll hook up with the other black person in the house.
But if it's like, ten per week,
I have a boyfriend back home.
And are we talking well liquor or top shelf?

The viewers want me
at a three-drink minimum, my forehead dipped
in Russian gasoline.
After the ceremony, West Coast viewers are invited
to complimentary punch and handshaking
on the church patio.
Later that night I wash up on an Atlantic beach,
push against Eastern screens
like an open mouth.

My dad used to watch and say I'd be perfect
and since I've started drinking
he says it louder. I make great television.

There isn't hope
but there is something
that happens when people on television
leave the house to go outside
and there is no background noise,
only colors brighter than the liquid
rolling in their stomachs.

I love my viewers as the sun—
the ones who watch me cuss in subtitles, teenage boys
mid-jerk, mothers who warn their daughters
but shine quietly, remembering,
siblings and cellmates
who don't speak during commercials,
odd couples, bad little kids, old people
who don't know how to change the channel,
viewers who are stoned,
hopped up, buttered, hungry, wasted,
full of acid or chicken or shit.
Give me a drink and I will do a service.

Greetings from Struggle City

1

I do the human being thing
leave curtains open for the rats
suck the teat of basic cable   especially commercials

I like to make white people laugh
compare tattoos with strangers on Chat Roulette
and drink to them in limbo

I'm legs crossed on the plastic-covered sofa
All green with morality I roll on living
(impetus being adventure or getting laid)

Stable   says mother when it's warm enough
to leave the window open while I sleep
on the marble floor   accidental genesis couplet

Lately it's a mirror image of myself as teenager
straddling a middle-management type with a bony
butt   crying over two-minute punk B-sides

What is that thing   A beak   And what
is attached to it   And do you ever get tired of
keeping your tongue to yourself

2

If a lover visits, take him first into the kitchen,
offer wedges of something dipped in angel stench.
He might thank you much later by nesting
at the base of your neck, warding blind cats away.
A flyer stuck to my seat on the train asks
Where will you spend eternity?
Moving is always such a bitch.
Today Sagittarius will experience changes
in the romantic sphere. So, like, that's cool.
If you want a do-right-all-day woman
like me, a warm darling who steps over puddles,
tongue of sky and a helluva cook, decked
out in flesh and bones and harps,
you've gotta have fingernails like veins.
One animal lies down next to another and nearby

some bulbs are leaning in the wind.
You are welcome to touch my real estate.

3

Self-portrait as Jay Z

Sleepy as a motherfucker
Tall as burning bush   Man I'm high
                                                        enough to shoot
with no hands   change my name
            after revolution   knock down
he who does not feel me
            make that shit look easy

If   we all hustlers
            in love with the same thing
why are my people strung
                                                up on clothing lines
why   means necessary

Have you heard
            I come from the streets
I hustle harder   but look better from behind

I'll fucking murder you, pig!!!!   For something
to do with my mouth   [then everyone laughs,
their shoulders bob up
            and down in tweed blazers]

4

When the snow comes
you come
For a taste of your neck I would
burn my tongue
I want to look my best
crawling across nicked wood
sobbing for my people
their most desirable meats sliced
with a glass of tomatoes and ants
Sagittarius replies *yes please*
in matters of the heart

doesn't knock the hustle
never feels
she is asking too much
I would take you into the kitchen and kiss you
necks just close enough to stove burners
Now where the fuck is my letter

5

A funny thing that happened last week is: I read that Mos Def does a
fantastic impression of Bob Holman! It was finally sunny so I played
hooky from work. Got my boots re-soled, wished I had Kim Gordon's
eyebrows, picked up the Shaft soundtrack along with some weird Walt
Whitman vinyl with a naked dude on the cover. It's pretty good but
I've never heard of the guy reading the poems and the music in the
background is hit or miss. Some of it is kind of wack. I don't know if Walt
would have been down with it.

6

I climb your shoulders
as a white sky bear,
cover the veins
of your neck in soot.
From the cracked window:
a thin skin
of politeness. Winds
are dry, twenty-five
to thirty anxieties.
We cast echoes, sip
gimlets. Grasshoppers
feast on us.

7

In most of these stories I am naked:

At an art gallery I am denied free wine
or Don discovers me one morning
making eggs and is embarrassed by my tits.
For a week back then we had nothing
but beer in both fridges, some hard cheese.
I was naked when the cops came

and Don said they were just mad
they couldn't have a joint.
When they left he passed a few around the room,
everyone in underwear listening to Marvin Gaye.

8

If you really want to know
I dropped a carrot
on the floor making soup
tripping over a Snuggie
covered in cigarette ash
No   I want the future here now
while my arms are still inked up
Where are your balls Morgan
says my brother I mean
I swear you have some
And the last man
with an accordion jumps
from a rooftop because
his family left him
between commercials
You know the one
with the chicken nuggets
That's my favorite
In the kitchen with eggs
and tomatoes I am scratching
my legs and feeling independent
I leave the carrot for the dog
He touches it to his dark mouth
I push a little sermon on them
Things are terrible again
A couple on the train whispers
Kings moths and oak trees
snow-colored
I follow you like a puppy
to its own asshole
I nurse my wine glass
This eternity of pepper
and rosemary   will you
spend it indoors?

There Is Another World and I Am Better in It

In which brother removes my eardrum
and lightbugs nest in its place

Other things are Christmas lights
and thin film strips how it feels

to be wrapped up now I believe
this was a prophecy of men

fresh flowers on the table short black
dresses on fire escapes across America

Is it all right to encounter people
this way with fear Jeff's here again

and we have a kid a doll we keep
in the car while we fuck in the backseat

Have I memorized the West or are these
dream highways from another night

How it feels to keep digging in
my pockets but nothing is there

Our kid gets out of line Jeff tells her
never to disappear again

I remain near sleep to finish
up a monologue enter the houses

of television families and eat
their bagels for breakfast

I stare at the blinds I check my temperature
Hundreds of hands open and close

They can feel me
I get up to piss realize I am out of bagels

In Search of Morgan, Season 3, Episode 24

I'm wading through a lot of family
bullshit to find her
different-colored visitor to *The Cosby Show* house
who caught my pregnant mother's ear
So there I was

ad-libbed and already losing my hair
I slithered but did not crawl

This many Decembers later
I still hope men aren't looking at my face
I sob in the middle of the night for false arrests
Let prescription dosage and cup size increase
as dark-shouldered sisters

Brother got grandpa's name tacked on early
But I was plucked from primetime cable
They say you can find Morgan if you are moving
at a rate of thirty-four hugs per season
If she does not exist, I do not exist

Every morning I scrape hymns from the backs
of my teeth
Vodka, very dry, three olives
Morgan will you please come when I call
I am a name sucking chai from its bag
I am a terrible liar and always cold

What does black family look like
when educated with masses
Sometimes I pass for delightful
And Theo, I am watching your hair

I get down with spinoff-era Denise
Suit up in black coffee perfume
Drip-dry my liver on the fire escape
I am president of the societies for
No More Pretty Girls Writing Poems
No More Clothes in Summer
Morgan only the biggest peaches for you

Cliff is taking Rudy and her friends out to lunch
at a fancy restaurant
Morgan, 6, says, *Mr. Huxtable you look so handsome*
This would be the first clue

No More Kissing Sounds from Men on Street
No More White Girl Problems
Morgan, believe me, I get sunburns too
I am an unstable hair color
I associate waiting with being dead

Rudy and her friends are not happy with their food
Morgan eats all the olives
even though she is allergic

ON GETTING ONE'S GROOVE BACK

Touching you on the shoulder
is the most honest I've been
all week. Desire,
round and troubling,
fits softly under skin.
I write one and a half
on a chalkboard
meaning, for example, a man I love
is in the room but he is not
touching me. If I moan louder
will it encourage you?
Do you understand how the ocean
contains like a box?
Last night M planned
to stop drinking for a while because
he is getting fat
and also because of the pills.
He sees symbolism
in his ex-boyfriend,
carries genes of the divine.
Even Don wants to move on.
It's because of 9/11
that he's so goddamn
political. He cries
on my left sleeve
about his uncle,
the altered
emotional psyche
of our generation.
Says it isn't just the beer.
This morning I feel my head
getting screwed back on,
blood more solid.
I need to be touched
while the dogs twitch and snore
wishing for something drastic,
sweet and full of color.
No one hears
when I am spoken.

MISS BLACK AMERICA

Does she flat-iron
or out-of-package relaxer

Does she blow out   pick clean
shape up   or flip her weave

Does she got that good hair
from her mama's side

Does she let her
white friends touch

Is she style and grace
Is she dy-no-mite

Is she a doll for you   does she come
with a special comb

Everyone Knows Where Art Comes from
It Comes from the Store
for Keith Haring

I'm telling you *it's in the hips*,
the cash you cut and sniff
over my horn-rimmed cartoon,
walls shaking like DayGlo
and LES nightclub
toilet I'm pulling my face from.
Behind the stall you draw our outlines
on a scratched-up mirror with
red lipstick you took from my purse.
And suddenly it's like penises everywhere.
Surfing new wave airwaves
you shout, *Are we not men?* But you
are drowned out, drooling a pool
of screenprints to the floor. A: We are
empty! Hollow as egg whites
and ink between our eyes. Wouldn't
you know it? Crack pipes no longer
pass for sexy fingers. Turns out
everyone's empty as sin and
heads are televisions, empty too.
Still, I'd let any man
paint me into a corner
these days with a good set of lips.
In this equation everyone stands for me.
Oh you in your strikened pose!
Oh fly honey baby
on the run and on the market!
It's like pictures are words
or sex is a Xerox machine.
It's like all my friends are fucking
in a planet-sized circle around me.
You're what I think I see
on the G train platform, glowing
womb spiked with the glory
of everyone, but then wake up again.
I know a little something about pissing
in public but nothing about loving.
It's funny because there are 1,700 products
stamped just for you, rising from cinderblock
murals to meet you at the checkout
line in the sky. Say, Mister, are you for sale?

I think I become for sale too, become
the greatest hits or a seed of greatest hits,
lock the door to my stall and drip plastic
over the boredom, the pills, the patent
leather, the chunks of hair in the sink.
When the party ends I will still
be here with you, lips stained with pop.
I could pick a billion flowers for your sick bed.
Do you see me I could dance all night

APOLOGY WITH PEARLS ON

Isn't it enough that I am in bed
with Digable Planets, silk pajamas?

Was going to say *shitty*, got
auto-corrected. Took back

leopard print, inserted
houndstooth. I am moving

on up, getting dee-luxed.
Cleaning the house without

your tongue. Not rolling
in my six-four toward

anywhere. Green hills, wild blue
what you're thinking

I can also think. If I want I can
cross my legs, or hush.

Make *darling* less sharp.
I whittle down to lace

stockings, get laser-removed.
Skip dollar-Bud Thursday to slink

along the Chelsea circuit white-wined.
I'll take this one: Graceful and gold-tipped

I point to culture, no pop all fizzle.
To canvas, a savings account with truffles.

Think eggshell white, stainless
gums clenched. Uptightening

in sonatas I call home. Finally
planting basil, patient to save you

a sprig. Improved, I ask
instead of take.

Rest Stop / Fresno County Line / January

The rain is sudden
and hard. I am
writing this
after sunset. I am
resolving to
stick to my own kind. I
wish you
unkeepable
resolutions. I wish you
difficulties
in bed with
older women.

Tomorrow I must
check on the shore-
line, make
sure blueness has
not moved.
I lost
balances
and ceremonies
in the cold. They were
swept up
with leaves
from the pavement.

I am writing this
with half-
letters.
You are the letters
of my name
inversed. I
ask the
long French braid
of stability to
lead
me to
lemonade
stands in winter. You
are in my
way.

White Walls White People

"To Whites every Black holds a potential knife behind the back, and to every Black the White is concealing a whip." –René Ricard, in a profile of Jean-Michel Basquiat, Artforum 1981

the nerds today   are rich   and proud   of cutting-edge
mission statements on white   letterhead they've been
        doing some thinking   about what lunch
says about who they are   do they look whiter
in this sandwich?   they don't date outside it would be too
     complicated they don't want to tell me about
their black friends but they do

hell, let's look at the theory   college was very important

I'm not here
to teach them but I am

       look at me looking at art
supporting the local opening the eyes   of the public
     see how when I hang black
         on my white walls   it's fine

     the nerds get turned on   by the race
meanwhile I   white light/white heat
my way down   the block I walk hard

they're impressed with my work   I've *lived*
     I am very Afro-centric   they make pictures
where lips are faces and in them the dark is what stands out

     the way *funky*   leaves their lips
the way they've framed what I've framed

sometimes things are simple   sidewalks
acrylic and white oil

I see something   when I close my eyes
     looking at it
       I feel strange   let's let it exist
out of my way   like a drinking fountain

I pour coffee out of my mug
while I'm washing it the handle breaks

Young, Sassy, and Black

I use these words
to distract you.

Quiet Alcohol

It is our usual holiday.
You ask if you can trouble me for a glass
of whiskey. Someone asks me offhand
about the hate in my spine. I say,
Fuck babies, and *My mother*
didn't like the flowers I bought her
and *Do you see what I mean?*
My mother is always a different person.
These are standard answers. But lately
in pale light I examine bruises
I hope are from you, teach myself mechanics
of clear evenings and I am
steeped in insults for you.
I want quiet alcohol
untouched by light and fingertips,
settled safely under half-moon,
crests dilating with slow breath.
There are no feelings here
and I do not want to go home. Soon
we will be underwater, life forms
in air pockets. And I do not trust
this place to scoop us up, teach us
to move, hips following current,
arms like pillars expanding and stretching
under highway glow. You know
I always cry at holidays.

On Children, How I Hate Them and Want to Corrupt Them, How You Know I Hate Them, and What That Could Mean

What they preach in Clark County is false.
In the air, we are only negation. Someone says,
Our seat cushions are also floatation
devices! And home is also a vacation spot
where potions are served hot and good and we fill
our noses with the stuff of life-sized plastic. Before takeoff
I watch the sun reflecting in the snow. A tiny slice
of brick wall glows and I fall asleep smiling. Somewhere
in Jersey the children inquire about syllables.
The children are small units who need to be controlled.
Tiny wrists and spines are stacks of hardened smoke.
Two pairs of manic eyes make their way
toward me. One set of red palms squeezes my knees.
The one in the pink dress has a fish
named something that reminds her of my earrings.
She puts a spell on me, quietly, but I see her eyelashes
drip to the floor one by one. I accidentally think
about the best ways to make you spread my legs.
Later that night, I'm almost passed out on a stolen hotel comforter,
licking ashy tongues to hell's ice caps, watching the news
on a flatscreen: Losses Sting Male Ego. I decide to write
a chick flick. I already have one scene and it's about you.
In a bar somewhere a girl says to Joe, *I don't remember*
a word of French. At the other side of the counter,
across from three vodka sodas, the chick's friends ask her
about last night. The chick is definitely Kate Hudson.
She tells her chicks the sex was *earnest.* She takes a sip
and her eyelids dissolve. Somewhere in Jersey, the wood house
cowers around me like a smell. Bridges line the town.
Their jaws are swans, arching deep sleeping backs to rainfall.
This is how your fingers ask my thighs.
On the patio we watch our sleep fall into yellow beer
like food coloring. I suspect the children know you can't
be aggressive in bed without laughing.
I know you represent the storm: low-ceilinged
and distributed to the night. Our torsos are poised
in the clouds. A few vines serve as litter in the dark.
You sink behind a ditch of moths. Children know there is a trick
about the wind, twelve seconds before it rains.

Miss Black America

Is she brushstroke   or installation
Is her gown   out of season

Is her necklace made of blood
Diamonds from Sierra Leone chorus

played back as her sash
hangs   like a strange   heavy fruit

Has she dreamed of this day
since the moon was blue

Is she the window   and the breaking
of the window

Does she neo-expression
her way out of the hood

I'd Rather Sink . . . Than Call Brad for Help!

Fucking Brad! He isn't
wondering but if
he is I'm cold and I'm
black like someone
else's sky my ugly
face fresh-baked
cookies like I lost
my damn
first love
this fall is
weekly now I'm
taking wood floors
and carpets in place
of his ghostly hand
dialing nothing what
a life! I think all I'm
pissing at this point
is liquor I can barely
see anymore can't
count to channel
eighteen I slip
into a sea of red
leather Brad if you're
out there I am
doing just fine
iced lashes and all
sloppy underslept
waves getting the job
done I let them
into my mouth they taste
better than you would
incidentally I'm too old
for weekends already
I've never worked out
in my work-out clothes
I'd rather my lips peel
right off into a glass
of warm white wine this
is the mushy part as far as
Brad is concerned I'm
glamour as usual
I could be dropped

dead just think
of all the money I'd save
and time! Drifting smoothly
with my belly full
head in the sink no hair
left at all waking up
in a warmer place I'd
call it unbaptism

THE GREAT PACIFIC GARBAGE PATCH

At the time I was trying
to have out-of-body
experiences and husbands
My mouth was dry
for attention I flipped
up my skirt for a little sun

On the coldest days
when sunsets turned to milk
I slept a little longer

Hold my hand under the table

*

For now we are taking
someone's grandma's pills
I am slicing a wedge of brie
with a comically large blade
We walk a windy canyon and are safe
Someone asks where that blood on the floor came from

*

This kitchen table is the only place
Maybe we have been here for days
While the animals shake
we write our names in marker
on the old wood

When I am not
reminding myself I am remembering

which is worse
because our fingers smell like flowers
because kitchen tables are made for eating
fucking, snorting

Like the small feeling never left I wake up

*

We think our fingers
smell like flowers but it is only opium

Let us go slowly on this path of being
Let us wake up in different beds

Everyone is talking

trash stew

There's a lot of praying going on
in these hills here

*

We float   the way hair fills plastic bags
the way these states are heading underwater
into hills as expensive as our mouths

We don't touch   watch from the window
Then sunshine for an hour

Something in the sky
moves sideways and too fast

You are the jesus of this room

Hot Serpent in the City

Now it is afternoon dear
god another bird dead head
in a snow pile dull claws
in the air it would have said
if it could talk what the fuck
but snow was in our mouths
frigid tongues
getting a little rest
shallow planets kept warm
by paychecks and fig trees
reeking on my fingers I stored
your ribs in the icebox
next to the frozen meatballs
if you need them and so on
and so on white in my mouth
nothing in the sky nothing
blooming I forget names
of colors the way they
measure bodies what's this one
dressed as a silken drum
thinks it can push me around
lives in a field of new wings
lives under a great sea
a city block unfolds slowly
in our mouths just simple
outlines nothing remarkable
if you're curious bite down
a little harder on your lips
count body parts til you can
sleep forearm wrist nipple
temple the world
is no place for an angel
normally this is where you
would interject take a little walk
around the garden touch the spines
of animals as you pass just like that
I say come on all these churches
their thirty bells can't even
get us clean what's this color
whispering on the sidewalk
stretching out like a slanted cloud
and so on olive-lipped I flirt

with some matches a clay bone
at dawn demons pour into
storm drains as bitter wine

proverbs hush up
you don't give a damn

POEM

I know it takes seven years for our cells to change
so I started last Thursday the train
was pregnant with stillness and groceries so
do you know what I thought? I wondered
and then I thought I would be sick
with the sound of your feet against hardwood
coming to sweep up twisted spine
with that thing you always say and the way you always
say it you say you'll get it right next time
thinking it's my fault so I read some June Jordan
poems caught you hiding in the margins begging
to be swallowed got off two stops early nauseous
later that night I'm so anxious I knit
two rows of a scarf it's so ugly I fall asleep

Poem

We're already behind schedule so I wait under
a ledge and watch the first snow of the month
it lasts approximately three minutes
when the bus finally pulls in the driver tells me
the turnpike is at a dead stop and when I say
dead he says I mean faces are made up
of pulled clay rodents drift from wire rafters in this
bus its arched back tunneling found objects
that have nothing to do with Hartford CT and
everything to do with learning to count women
like Sappho cream cheese and black music in
the trees tonight it's all radio and they're all bare
I'm afraid to fall asleep drooling on the red carpet
seat so I crane my neck to watch the other cars
bundled tiny and safe crawling on repeat

MISS BLACK AMERICA

For her talent   does she work magic
part your lips and she   appears

Does she wish for world peace
equality   or has she given up

On the platform   is she for sale
     or a raised fist

Is she lathered in cocoa butter
under her swimsuit

Is her body filled up darker
     than blue   does it shine

in this light   will it still shine
     on her walk home   in the red air

For her crown does she get
40 acres   braided with cowrie

THEIR GRANDMOTHERS NEVER DID THE LAUNDRY
"Black people are the glory of a shared piece of candy." –William Pope.L

Their grandmothers never did the laundry.
My grandmother did it for them

for less than I make an hour
talking to them about paintings.

It was a simpler time.
Front lawns were pie and rum punch.

Some women were beautiful. My grandmother
wiped their pumps clean of fertilizer

or took their lipstick out of a lapel.
My platforms are always smeared

with dog shit, pencil skirts wrinkled
up against their white thighs at brunch.

In the bathroom where they wash
their hands there is a picture in a black

Pier 1 Imports frame. O! Let their bladders
be full of nostalgia for old New York.

There is no black in the pictures.
Where are all the slaves?

I dab, blot, lick. Did whoever
came before me eat chitlins for breakfast?

Stuff her black lips with hollandaise
and home fries and if she cried

into her cotton palms did the sky go black?
More importantly were there carnations

softening in a cup and out of frame does anyone
notice a shackle? I bet they don't.

The waitress will ask how I like my eggs.
I'll say scrambled but wish I said

black and tough as shit.

Epistolary Poem for Reader, Brother, Grandmother, Men (or, When I Say I Want to Spit You Up)

I'm thinking, what would happen
if I started masturbating on this subway car?

It's late. An African man next to me
is reading the president's book.

Drinks tonight with an older poet
who told me that Winnie the Pooh
is the same as Homer Simpson and
he is correct.

I have been leaving space
on one side of the bed
which gives me sad dreams.
(Reader, please know
when I say bed I mean sex.)

You give me a reason to get up
in the afternoon. To believe in
what elders call having church.

In my sleep I try to persuade you
to fall in love with me. I also do this
while watching Turner Classic Movies
and wishing I had enough
money for a country house.

I am infinitely comforted by thunder, how
it is connected to my dog,
growling in his sleep.
I am close to the darkness
of Lowell, Massachusetts, where women
have cried and worked.

Men in pants like that
holding my hands like that.

If I call you *brother*
instead of *bro*, it's because I am overtaken
by the need to enunciate and pronounce.

It does not mean you are my brother
who never calls me back
and most recently was featured in a dream
about a giant silver vagina,
the centerpiece of a parade.
Who did not recognize
the puffy costume as a vagina
because my unconscious prefers him to be
sexually inexperienced.

You might think this makes me nervous,
or concerned, the way mothers feel
when their children take too many
years to speak, but I'm not.

I am more comfortable
being mourned than loved.

I feel my death: It is tucked
inside my ear like an itch
or a bad idea.

It's too late for coffee, or reason, or capability.

Maybe if I knew my grandmother
and the white family she worked for,
I would feel different
about everything around me.

Instead I can only describe half
of the view outside the kitchen window.
Brown curtains are covering
the other half and I don't mind it.

The past has not been as rewarding
as I had hoped.

Instead it feels
like something dark and hard is back there.
I spit it up
like a stringy peach.

LOOK

"We're gonna have to do more than talk." –Fred Hampton

The nerds today are tall   and angry they are yelling
we want   paintings and books about paintings we want white
men with beards to explain that
           everything will be OK downtown
if they could make fists   where would they   go would they
stink of color   theories, ash   from offerings sent to reds
found in the hearts   of rocks crushed down

In the time of discovery and rules I was still foreshortened   but looking
at cubism these days   I get bored   I don't eat dinner
stay awake when it is quiet except for two nerds talking on the street below
they do not wonder   if what they are feeling is the same
as revolution   if entropy   has gotten stuck   their people were not
promised anything   it is easy for them to talk

If I could make a fist   I would make them see their good luck
how revolution is a privilege   and fun
we're all here, one says, *doing it*   if I could I would take some
        power for myself   they want books
four thousand pages in your name   you didn't have a choice
these days you are a dark stain still spreading on a mattress   under glass
If they could make a fist   they could see
          they don't know anything   or remember

For my anxiety   I will take   a mule and no big ideas
          for you I wonder if there is an end   if the end
is better   is something we have not yet seen   can't see
I can't get tired   am on watch   the nerds talk, talk, look
to canvas in frames   when they see red   it is a comfort
they are so goddamn sure

Blessings, Injuries

Sky opens over large charcoal bricks. Clouds
are puffed cheeks, tear-colored. It is sixteen
years ago and the cracked coffee pot slips
out of your head, down seven flights of stairs.
My brain is flower petals
and your fingers are strings. My breasts
are castle walls, your arm is a castle wall.
A garden sprouts an ear.
My face is covered in fruit flies.
We have a history of refusing to touch.

Everything Is Bothering Me

My therapist says
I remind her of Woody Allen
It sounds like something
out of a Woody Allen movie
a little peach-colored and rich

*

All my friends say *baby*
don't go to work tomorrow
I go home quietly
wake up and go to work
I can do it forever

*

We tried to see the meteor shower
from a cliff spit bourbon
out of flasks at the moon
you said you'd never disrupt space
I said hell I own it

*

Everything flesh-covered
colored in flesh
my sunken stomach
some billowy clouds

*

I am trying to sleep alone
you are doing whatever
I swear to god I know people
they live on the Internet
they are the best

*

The hills are large yellow dogs
trees on the mountains
turn to moss I wonder how
beneath me kitchen tiles
move quickly into next week

*

The street is quiet
for some reason
and someone is throwing up
maybe the ants
or the sunrise or the pavement

*

Dawn is foggy
an infinite blue stomach
a child
learning the function
of a verb

*

We are losing a war against
three-tiered houses they sink
their claws into the hill and bite
None of the right gods
will have me

*

Chorus of how you are
like milk or the shiver
of a little butter in a frying pan

*

I stalk buildings for you
like one word shoving another
I wait at a bar in the desert
drink three glasses
of yellow beer

*

I double as a canvas
for lit-up seeds
boys like fat brushstrokes
up close
they are grotesque

*

You ask me to cross the river
in the middle of the night
It occurs to me
the river
is roughly the size of your dick

*

In some non-Western myths
it is possible
for a woman to become a god
what I can do is give a good hug
open up what's in a pill

*

So I can be more present
I am getting emails on my phone
there are other places
ways of living
we have ruled them out

*

Advertisements are suddenly
not beautiful
I scrub my house
I let it get late

*

I've thought heavily
about the apocalypse
since I was eight years old but
I've never considered strategy except
to smoke cigarettes and wait

APOLOGY IN HOPES OF MEN

These days I'm looking good.
Voiced over
with a glossier me.
Wearing giggles
to the knee, keeping
elbows off your lungs
and out of the dirt. Half trying
to be secret, slip
into a room
unannounced. Glide softly
onto the couch and wait
for you to speak
first. Will you
hear me coming, pink
upper lip
to incense stick? Deep-cut
Aretha behind
the ears where synth
was planted once.
As a woman
I ignore what is
half-assed and full of water.
I understand
our troubles
passed down: I tuck them
into my loafers
and cross my legs. No complaints
here. I take my time.
I get excited
over time.
Hands to myself
as I am told.
No longer wonder what if
somehow a little mystery
could hurt. No longer swear
to god it's when
I'm dead
I will shut up.

OTHER PEOPLE'S COMFORT KEEPS ME UP AT NIGHT

for Ted Meyer

Today darling I am rising
from the lavender bathtub
of self-loathing. I don't take drugs
to shut up I take off
my pants when I get home
and I stay there, red cup full
of cigarettes from heaven, ghosts
of all my friends between my toes.
I imagine them pouring vodka all over
each other wearing glitter.
The vision is closing in like a tight dress.
Meanwhile the moon
fills gray-green. The shops in the village are
leaking bodies. Spilt oil rolls over
cash like hands, some glorious bullshit.
What bothers me is the weight
of clouds under your fire escape, your
hand strange lines I feel
and can't, one shared breath
of all the bulldogs in the park,
how I don't notice an inch below
something wriggling in dark warmth
as if love or hunger never counted
and I was never meant to last. The nervous
breakdown doesn't end.
It was only sleeping. And comes
back good and rested
smearing its eye boogers all over.
Says, *You're an arrogant prick.*
I say, *Fuck you nervous breakdown.*
It says, *Open the curtains and look
down at all the people* or
You may share your bed only with me.
I accidentally say *OK.*
When I can't sleep I smoke
a dark cigarette and keep the curtains closed
so I can lose track of where I am
and who is here with me. I cut the faces
out of magazines and pile them
in the middle of my hardwood floor.
In the distance, that good old
rock 'n' roll. This isn't simple
if you want it to be. What my country

does for me is enter
me like a room, becomes the furniture,
the wall, the painting on the wall,
the white spot where painting used to sing.
Singing enters me, becomes the window.
Baby think of my skin
as the best part of the song. Take me
by the ribs and lay me at the bottom
of a dirty creek where I can
get a good view.

OTHER PEOPLE'S ACKNOWLEDGEMENTS

Eternal gratitude to the editors who first published the following poems:

Why I Am Not A Painter: a gathering of poems by MFA students in NYC (Argos Books, 2011): "On Children, How I Hate Them and Want to Corrupt Them, How You Know I Hate Them, and What That Could Mean"

Phantom Limb: "There Is Another World and I Am Better in It"

Handsome: "The World Is Beautiful but You Are Not in It"

NOÖ Journal: "Poem [We're already behind schedule so I wait under]"

[PANK] Online: "If My Housemate Fucks with Me I Would Get So Real (Audition Tape Take 1)" and "Poem Made of Chewed-Up Nicorette from the Garbage in Front of Kate Hudson's House"

Painted Bride Quarterly: "Poem [I know it takes seven years for our cells to change]," "Apology with Pearls On," "Epistolary Poem for Reader, Brother, Grandmother, Men (or, When I Say I Want to Spit You Up)," "Boys, Boys, Boys," and "America This Is for You (Audition Tape Take 2)"

Vinyl Poetry: "I'm Not Like the King of Black People"

Forklift, Ohio: "I Was Trotting Along and Suddenly," "On Getting One's Groove Back" and "Morgan What, Morgan Who?"

ILK Journal: "Poem for the June Eclipse"

Coconut Poetry: "The Great Pacific Garbage Patch"

The Literary Review: "Look," "Real Housewife Defends Herself in Front of a Live Studio Audience" and "It Doesn't Get Cold Where We're from and We Weren't Taught"

No, Dear: "Miss Black America [Does she flat-iron]"

Vanitas: "White Walls White People"

Gigantic Sequins: "There Are Other Things I Want to Explain but They Are Mysteries"

Tin House: "Poem Made of Empty Prescription Bottles from the Garbage in Front of Bill Murray's House" and "Other People's Comfort Keeps Me up at Night"

Pinwheel: "Everything is Bothering Me"

Boog City: The Portable Boog Reader 7: "Miss Black America [does she drink]" and "Everyone Knows Where Art Comes from It Comes from the Store"

The Offending Adam: "Other People's Comfort Keeps Me up at Night," "How to Piss in Public and Maintain Femininity"

Blunderbuss: "Hot Serpent in the City"

Western Beefs of North America: "Greetings from Struggle City"

Apogee Journal: "Their Grandmothers Never Did the Laundry"

Group hug to the brilliant minds, other halves, relentless lovers, editors and supporters who helped make this book, including but not *at all* limited to: my great big perfect family, Ted Meyer, Clea Litewka, Josh Bell, Matthew Rohrer, Tracy K. Smith, Catherine Silver, Bruce Covey, Brenda Shaughnessey, Craig Teicher, Natalie Eilbert, Angel Nafis, Danez Smith, Charif Shanahan, Nate Marshall, Abba Belgrave, Zachary Bowman, my MoCADA family, and my all my peers and teachers at Columbia, NYU, and Cave Canem.

Thanks to Bravo, MTV, Jay Z, O'Hara, Brooks, Lichtenstein, Bill Murray, Biggie Smalls, Curtis Mayfield, Kate Hudson, etc., and whoever invented wine.

To the amazing Eileen Myles (who has long been an inspiration) for saying yes, and to Hanna, Whitney, Elle, Colleen and all the beautiful women of Switchback for the tremendous work and love and energy they put into this book.

To Mom, Dad and my best friend Thomas: you're my three hearts.

Morgan Parker is the author of *Other People's Comfort Keeps Me Up At Night* (Switchback Books 2015), selected by Eileen Myles for the 2013 Gatewood Prize, and *There Are More Beautiful Things Than Beyoncé* (Coconut Books 2016). She received her BA in Anthropology and Creative Writing at Columbia University and MFA in Poetry from NYU. Her poetry and essays have been featured in numerous publications as well as anthologized in *Why I Am Not a Painter* (Argos Books 2011) and *The BreakBeat Poets: New American Poetry in the Age of Hip-Hop* (Haymarket Books 2015). A Cave Canem fellow and poetry editor for *Coconut Magazine* and *The Offing*, she also contributes writing to *Weird Sister* and co-curates the Poets With Attitude (PWA) reading series with Tommy Pico. She lives in Brooklyn and at www.morgan-parker.com.